The Magic School Bus® PRESENTS Volcanoes and Earthquakes

Scholastic Inc.

Photos ©: Alamy Images: 18 bottom right (Bjorn Svensson), 8 top left (Martin Siepmann/imageBROKER), 17 center left (Ragnar Th Sigurdsson/Arctic Images), 24 top left (Robert Gilhooly); AP Images/Corey Ford/Stocktrek Images: cover; Corbis Images: 12 (Alberto Garcia), 4–5 (Bruno Morandi), 29 top left (Jim Sugar), 18 top left (Martin Jones), 28 top right (Tim Davis); Dreamstime: 14 bottom right (Pawel Opaska), 15 (Sverimage); Flickr/Sam Beebe, Ecotrust: 8 bottom right; Getty Images: 9 (Alexander Fortelny), 13 bottom left (Andrea Rapisarda Photography), 28 top left (Carsten Peter), 19 (@iksanaimagery), 4 top left (Jaime Razuri/AFP), 3 bottom, 27 (Liu Jin/AFP), 26 bottom (Nicholas Kamm/AFP), 28 bottom right (Tom Nevesely), 1 (Werner Van Steen); iStockphoto/erlucho: 26 top left; Nature Picture Library: 3 center, 24–25 (Aflo), 14 top left (Paul D Stewart); Science Source: 22 (Carl Frank), 31 top right (David R. Frazier), 31 bottom left (Detlev van Ravenswaay), 3 top, 6 (Dr. Juerg Alean), 10 top left (Frans Lanting/MINT Images), 23 bottom (James King-Holmes), 30 (Jeremy Bishop), 20 bottom right (Kees Veenenbos), 17 bottom right (OAR/National Undersea Research Program), 20 top left (U.S. Geological Survey), 21 (Walter Myers); Seapics.com/Doug Perrine: 16; Superstock, Inc.: 29 bottom right (Aldo Pavan/age fotostock), 7 bottom left (Ben Cooper/Science Faction), 10–11 (José Fuste Raga/age fotostock), 24 bottom (Norbert Wu), 29 top right, 29 bottom left (Tips Images), 28 bottom left (Westend61); Thinkstock/Ernst Laursen: 13 center.

ISBN 978-0-545-68584-9

Produced by Potomac Global Media, LLC

All text, illustrations, and compilation © 2015 Scholastic Inc.
Based on The Magic School Bus series © Joanna Cole and Bruce Degen
Text by Tom Jackson Illustrations by Carolyn Bracken
Consultant: Dr. Douglas Palmer, science writer and lecturer, Institute of
Continuing Education, Cambridge University, England
Published by Scholastic Inc., 557 Broadway, New York, NY 10012.

12 11 10 9 8 7 6 5 4 3 2 1   15 16 17 18 19/0

Cover design by Paul Banks
Interior design by Carol Farrar Norton
Picture research by Sharon Southren

Printed in the U.S.A.   40
First printing, January 2015

Contents

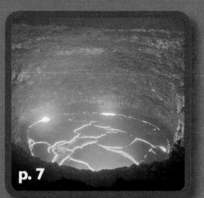

p. 7

p. 24

p. 27

Volcanic Zones

Earthquakes often occur in volcanic zones. They can make the ground shake so much that roads break apart.

Hop on the bus," Ms. Frizzle said. "Today we're going to places where rocks can melt and the ground can shake." She told us to look out for volcanoes. Wanda spotted some down below, all in a line. The Friz explained that they form along deep cracks in Earth's surface.

Is it safe to visit volcanoes, Ms. Frizzle?

Yes, it's safe, as long as we don't get too close. It's hard to predict when a volcano will erupt.

Smoking crater
The crater at the top of a volcano gives out steam, gases, and sometimes, hot lava.

Deep pipe
A pipe runs down through the volcano to deep underground. It's so hot down there that the rocks have melted.

Deep stuff!

How do volcanoes form?
by Wanda

Earth's surface, or crust, is broken into huge chunks called plates. Many volcanoes occur where the plates meet. Where plates move apart, hot liquid rock (magma) squirts up through the crack to create a new volcano. And when one plate is pushed below another, rock melts and rises to form a new volcano.

plate 1 ···· volcanic eruption
···· magma
···· plate 2

Frizzle Fact
Indonesia has 167 active volcanoes, more than any other country. In the last 300 years, there have been more than 1,000 eruptions there.

A Lake of Lava

A volcano has a hollow called a crater at the top. Some craters—like this one at Erta Ale, Ethiopia—have lava lakes inside them. Chunks of rock float on the surface.

Lava reaches 1,300 degrees Fahrenheit (700 degrees Celsius) — that's hot enough to melt soda cans.

When a volcano erupts, it sometimes releases a red-hot liquid called lava. Lava bubbles up from deep underground, where temperatures are high enough to melt rocks. Belowground, the red liquid is called magma. It's only called lava once it comes out of a volcano.

Lava is so hot, it's cool!

What's in lava?
by Phoebe

Lava is a hot liquid that contains a mixture of gas and chemicals that harden to form mineral crystals when they cool down. The minerals include silica, which makes sand crystals, and feldspar, which can turn into clays and mud. Depending on what minerals are in the lava, it can be runny and fast-flowing, or thick and sticky.

Lava cools to form volcanic rock, such as basalt. As basalt cools down, it forms long pipes and columns.

Basalt is very hard. Ancient Egyptians used it to make statues.

Frizzle Fact

There are only four lava lakes in the world today. The oldest, at the summit of Erta Ale, Ethiopia, has existed since 1906.

Shield Volcano

A lava bomb is a thick lump of rock that blasts out of a volcano. As it flies through the air, it cools and becomes partly solid.

A volcano does not start out as a mountain. Each eruption makes it grow. When the lava cools down, it becomes solid rock—and a new layer of the mountain. Some of the biggest volcanoes are shield volcanoes.

Lava domes are formed when the lava is less runny. They are steep because the thick lava cools before it flows far.

Shield volcanoes erupt more often than other volcanoes. Each eruption wipes out all life on the mountain.

Now that's BIG!

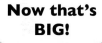

Where are Earth's biggest volcanoes?
by Ralphie

The biggest volcano on Earth is a shield volcano called Tamu Massif. It's on the seafloor of the Pacific Ocean. Its summit is 6,500 feet (1,980 meters) under the water, and the mountain is so wide it would cover the whole state of Oregon.

The largest land volcano is Mauna Kea on Hawaii. It rises 13,679 feet (4,169 meters) into the sky and contains enough rock to fill Lake Superior six times!

During an eruption, a jet of runny lava blasts out of the crater. It flows in all directions, creating a round mountain with a crater in the middle.

Stratovolcano

When we think of volcanoes, most of us picture a stratovolcano. It's a tall, steep, cone-shaped mountain with a flat top—that's where the crater is. When a stratovolcano erupts, it releases clouds of hot ash, shattered rocks, and thick, lumpy lava. The lava doesn't get far from the crater before it cools into solid rock.

Sometimes the center of a volcano collapses, creating a hollow area called a caldera.

That's Mount Fuji, in Japan—one of the biggest stratovolcanoes in the world. It last erupted about 300 years ago.

Ka-boom!

How do volcanoes grow so fast?
by Keesha

A stratovolcano can form a huge mountain really quickly. Mount Fuji took just 10,000 years to grow into Japan's tallest mountain (12,389 feet/3,776 meters). It takes normal mountains millions of years to get that high.

Stratovolcanoes have two types of eruptions. Slow, quiet eruptions add a layer of lava to the mountainside. Loud, explosive eruptions lay down a thick blanket of ash and rock.

Frizzle Fact
In 2013, an erupting volcano rose out of the ocean near Japan. The tiny island was called Nii-jima. A few months later, it was ½ mile (800 meters) wide.

Explosion!

That cloud can outrun any car, but not our Magic School Bus!

BOOM!

A cloud of hot ash and gas mixed with lumps of rock races down the side of the mountain, covering everything in its path.

olcanoes produce the biggest explosions the world has ever seen. Gases and magma build up under the mountain for many years, until the top of the mountain blows apart. The force of the explosion blasts solid rock into a cloud of hot dust.

Ancient city lost!

What happened at Pompeii?
by Dorothy Ann

Pompeii was an ancient Roman city located at the base of Mount Vesuvius, a volcano in western Italy. The people of Pompeii believed that Vesuvius wasn't dangerous. It hadn't erupted for years. About 2,000 years ago, in 79 CE, the mountain began to produce smoke, but the local people were not worried. Then the mountain exploded and the entire city of Pompeii — and 16,000 people who lived there — were buried in a huge cloud of ash and rock!

Volcanic clouds from the eruption of Vesuvius buried Pompeii — and its people — beneath 82 feet (25 meters) of ash. The city has since been excavated.

The cloud from an erupting volcano can reach more than 10 miles (16 kilometers) into the sky. That's far higher than any aircraft flies.

Frizzle Fact

The 1883 eruption of Krakatoa, near Java, could be heard 3,000 miles (4,830 kilometers) away in Perth, Australia.

Geysers

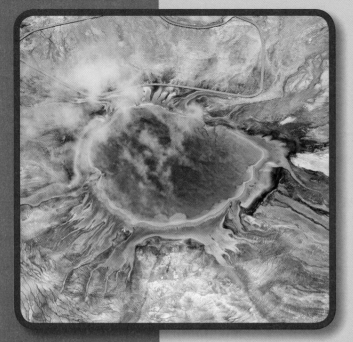

Bacteria living in hot, volcanic springs give the water a range of bright colors.

Lava and explosions are not the only strange phenomena in volcanic areas. These places also have geysers—natural fountains of water and steam that come to the surface as hot springs and boiling mud. Some geysers shoot high into the sky. More than half the geysers in the world are in Yellowstone National Park in Wyoming.

Boiling Mud

Bubbles
Hot steam and other gases rise up through the mud, making the surface bubble.

Mudpot
Hot mud is a mixture of water, gas, minerals, and other chemicals. It sometimes smells like rotten eggs.

Frizzle Fact
The world's tallest geyser is Steamboat Geyser in Yellowstone National Park. It reaches 300 feet (90 meters) into the sky.

The world's most famous geyser is Old Faithful at Yellowstone National Park. It got its name because it spouts faithfully every 90 minutes or so.

Steaming!

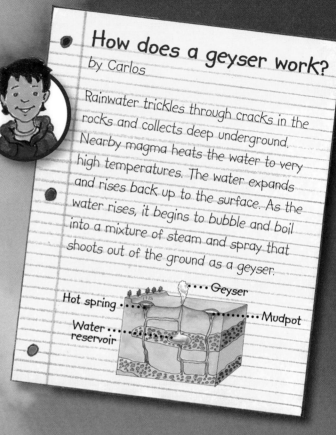

How does a geyser work?
by Carlos

Rainwater trickles through cracks in the rocks and collects deep underground. Nearby magma heats the water to very high temperatures. The water expands and rises back up to the surface. As the water rises, it begins to bubble and boil into a mixture of steam and spray that shoots out of the ground as a geyser.

Hot spring···· ···· Geyser

Water reservoir···· ···· Mudpot

Old Faithful squirts out enough water to fill 100 bathtubs!

The spray shoots up 15 stories high!

Undersea Volcanoes

New crust is made as Earth's plates move apart.

Red hot
Lava is hot when it erupts from the seafloor, but the cold ocean water quickly turns it into solid rock.

Most volcanic eruptions happen underwater on the seafloor. Undersea volcanoes are called seamounts. They erupt in the same way as volcanoes do on dry land. Most of the Earth's new crust is formed in volcanic zones in the ocean.

Crusty stuff!

How does new crust form?
by Arnold

New crust forms when Earth's plates move apart and vast cracks appear in the seafloor. Lava fills in the cracks and cools into a new bit of crust. Each eruption causes seafloor spreading — that is, when the newest bit of seafloor pushes the older crust out of the way.

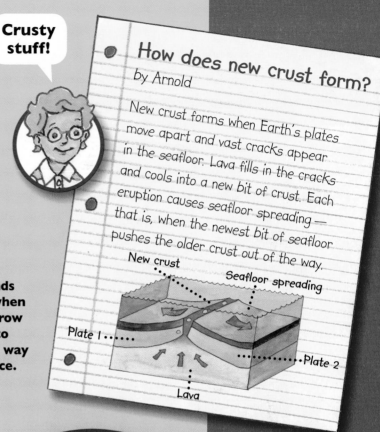

New crust

Seafloor spreading

Plate 1

Plate 2

Lava

Volcanic islands are formed when seamounts grow tall enough to reach all the way to the surface.

These round seafloor rocks are called pillow lavas.

Undersea eruptions produce rounded rocks. They cool quickly on the outside, but the lava inside takes longer to solidify.

Ancient Volcanoes

An active volcano is one that has erupted in the last 10,000 years.

Edinburgh Castle in Scotland is built on an extinct volcano. It last erupted 350 million years ago.

Most volcanoes erupt only every few hundred years. Between eruptions, a volcano is said to be dormant. Eventually, a volcano stops erupting altogether. Then it is described as an extinct volcano. There are many more extinct volcanoes than active ones.

Ngorongoro Crater in Tanzania, Africa, is the caldera of a volcano. It is incredibly big and covers 100 square miles (260 square kilometers).

Frizzle Fact

The Stromboli volcano in Italy has been erupting more or less continuously for over 2,000 years.

The Ball's Pyramid is all that remains of a huge shield volcano in the Pacific Ocean.

Where do the mountains go?
by Dorothy Ann

After they have stopped erupting, extinct volcanoes begin to erode. Solid rock cracks and crumbles into small grains that get carried away by wind and rain. This takes many millions of years.

The outer rocks of volcanoes are made from ash and lava. This type of rock is soft and erodes more quickly than the harder rocks inside. The hard rock you see here once filled the pipes and tubes in the middle of the volcano.

Volcanoes in Space

Io, a moon of Jupiter, is the most volcanically active place in the solar system.

Earth is not the only planet that has volcanoes. In fact, the largest volcano ever found is Olympus Mons, on Mars. At 374 miles (602 kilometers) across, it's as wide as Arizona. Some volcanoes in space emit lava, while others give out dust, ice, and steam. The dark patches on the surface of the Moon were made by huge volcanic eruptions hundreds of millions of years ago.

Olympus Mons is a shield volcano. It's 14 miles (22 kilometers) high, although its sides are not very steep.

Olympus Mons is nearly three times the height of Mount Everest.

Triton, one of Neptune's moons, is made mostly of ice. Its volcanoes erupt water and other liquids instead of liquid rock.

Martian mountains!

Why are Mars's volcanoes so big?
by Keesha

The surface of Earth is different from the other planets. Our crust is broken into plates that move around. As the plates move, the volcanoes move along with them, shifting away from the magma that makes them erupt. Eventually, all Earth's volcanoes will become extinct. Mars's crust is a single rocky shell. Its volcanoes don't move. They just keep erupting—and getting bigger and bigger.

Eruptions from geysers on Triton can last as long as a year.

This space suit is keeping me cozy.

Cracks in the Surface

This crack was created by an earthquake.

The two halves of the field moved in different directions.

Fault lines, like this one in Peru, are where earthquakes happen.

Next, Ms. Frizzle brought the bus near a fault line. "Earthquakes are caused by movements along faults, or cracks, in the ground," she told us. Faults occur where rocks finally break apart as pressure builds up in Earth's crust. The rocks break with a jolt, which sends shock waves through the ground. When these waves hit the surface, they make it shake violently.

Slow but steady!

Gives me the shakes!

What makes the ground move?
by Tim

The forces that push plates into each other, creating earthquakes, are the same ones that power volcanoes. Deep inside Earth, hot, thick, liquid magma churns around. The rocky plates of the crust float on top and are slowly pushed around by the magma. The plates only move 1 inch (2.5 centimeters) or so every year. However, even tiny movements create huge shock waves as two plates push together, pull apart, or slide past each other.

A machine called a seismograph picks up the shock waves from an earthquake. Scientists use the results to measure the earthquake and find where it started.

Frizzle Fact
Three-quarters of all earthquakes occur around the coastline of the Pacific Ocean.

Mighty Tsunamis

A tsunami is a giant wave created by an earthquake on the seafloor. When the seafloor moves, it creates ripples in all directions—just like when you drop a stone in a pond. The ripples from an earthquake are enormous. When they reach the coastline, they can cause terrible damage on land.

This ship was washed onto a house by a tsunami. Waves wash far inland, covering dry areas in deep water before running back into the sea.

地震 津波
CAUTION TSUNAMI HAZARD AREA
すぐに高い所へひなん
伊東市

Large tsunamis are very rare, but they can affect many people. Warning systems detect seafloor earthquakes. Signs tell people what to do when a tsunami comes.

Wave alert!

How do tsunamis grow so tall?
by Phoebe

Out in the deep ocean, a tsunami wave is hard to see. It is very wide and only a few feet (meters) higher than the surrounding water. The tsunami only rises up into a monster wave when it gets to the coast. Near shore, a big wave runs out of space in the shallow water, and so it pushes up above the surface of the water before crashing onto land.

Frizzle Fact
Tsunamis travel at speeds of about 500 miles (800 kilometers) per hour and can rise up to 130 feet (40 meters).

Earthquake!

As we drove back to school, the bus began to shake. "There's an earthquake happening right now!" shouted Ms. Frizzle. Deep underground, some rocks had ripped apart and the shock wave had reached the surface. It lasted for less than a minute, and then it was over. "Time to get back to class," said the Friz.

There are more than one million earthquakes around the world every year, but most are so small that people never feel them.

Around 100 earthquakes a year are strong enough to damage buildings. Some buildings are earthquake-proof — they are designed to not fall down.

Rescue teams use dogs to sniff out people trapped in buildings that have fallen down in an earthquake.

I'm shaking all over!

What is an epicenter?
by Carlos

Earthquakes occur several miles (kilometers) underground. The point on the planet's surface that is directly above the quake site is called the epicenter. This is where the earthquake is felt most strongly. The shock waves spread out from the epicenter in all directions and become weaker as they move farther away.

Epicenter·····

Quake site·····

Roads are built to be solid and stiff. When they are shaken by an earthquake, they crack apart.

Amazing Volcanoes

Mount Erebus

Mount Erebus is the nearest volcano to the South Pole. It is on an island near the coast of Antarctica. The 12,448-foot (3,794-meter) mountain is a young stratovolcano that has grown on top of an older shield volcano. The most active volcano in Antarctica, it has been erupting since 1972.

Mount Kilimanjaro

This volcano in Tanzania is the tallest mountain in Africa. It is 19,341 feet (5,895 meters) high, but not very steep. It's possible to walk to the summit.

Kilimanjaro has not erupted for at least 150,000 years, but scientists think it might become active at some point in the future.

Krakatoa

This volcano is a small island in Indonesia. It erupted in 1883, making both the largest eruption — and the loudest sound in recorded history. The entire island blew up. The ash cloud blocked out so much sunlight that the world grew colder for several months.

Mount St. Helens

This stratovolcano in Washington State used to be 9,677 feet (2,950 meters) tall. In May 1980, the top of the mountain exploded, leaving a massive crater. The eruption covered the surrounding area in a thick layer of ash. The mountain's summit is much lower now—8,365 feet (2,550 meters).

Kilauea

This mountain on the Big Island of Hawaii is probably the most active volcano in the world. Its main crater is a lake of lava called Pu'u 'O'o. During eruptions, fountains of lava form in the lake. Kilauea is the youngest of five huge volcanoes that make up most of the Big Island.

Well done, class! Let's get ready for our next adventure!

Mount Pinatubo

The 1991 eruption of Mount Pinatubo in the Philippines was the biggest volcanic event since the explosion of Krakatoa in 1883. Luckily, scientists figured out the mountain was about to erupt, and thousands of people were evacuated from the area just in time.

Mount Vesuvius

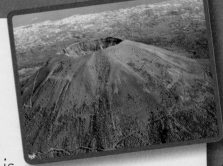

This stratovolcano on the west coast of Italy is famous for destroying the city of Pompeii. The mountain is still active — it's the most active volcano on the European mainland. It last erupted in 1944, and scientists are expecting it to erupt again in the near future.

Chimborazo

This mountain can claim to be Earth's tallest. Measured from sea level, it's lower than Everest. But it's close to the Equator, where the planet bulges outward. So the distance from the top of Chimborazo to the center of Earth is farther than the same distance for Everest.

Meet the Experts

Volcanoes pose a threat to people living in many parts of the world. One job for the scientists who study them is to figure out when the next eruption is going to happen. To do that, the experts have to understand what causes eruptions in the first place.

A vulcanologist goes up close to watch an eruption — but not too close!

〈 Vulcanologist

The people who study volcanoes are called vulcanologists. They wear silver suits that reflect the great heat from erupting lava. These scientists develop more reliable means of predicting eruptions. They check the temperature of the mountain and collect gases that come from the crater. They also make detailed maps of a volcano and can tell when it starts to bulge with magma long before it's apparent to the naked eye.

〉 Astrogeologist

An astrogeologist uses what he or she knows about the rocks on Earth to figure out how moons and other planets in the solar system are constructed. Space probes landing on alien worlds can detect earthquakes, while volcanic eruptions can be seen from space. These observations tell the scientists how alien worlds are similar to Earth, but also how they are different.

⌃ Seismologist

A seismologist collects data that helps us understand what the planet is made of deep down. The rocks beneath our feet are often very active and give out vibrations as they bend and break beneath the surface. Some of the biggest vibrations come from earthquakes. The vibrations from an earthquake travel as waves — a bit like the sound waves that travel through the air to our ears. But vibrations whizz through rock hundreds of times faster than they do in air. Scientists called seismologists pick up the vibrations from earthquakes to see how they change speed and even echo off objects far below the surface.

Words to Know

Caldera A hollow that forms when the center of a volcano collapses.

Clay A kind of earth that can be shaped when wet and baked to make bricks, pottery, or figures.

Crater The mouth of a volcano or geyser.

Crust The hard outer layer of Earth's surface.

Crystal A clear or nearly clear mineral or rock with many flat faces, such as quartz.

Dormant A volcano that's "sleeping" — not doing anything now, but could erupt again.

Equator An imaginary line around the middle of the Earth that is an equal distance from the North and South Poles.

Erode To wear away gradually by water or wind.

Erupt To throw out lava, hot ashes, and steam from a volcano, suddenly and violently.

Evacuate To move away from an area or building because it is dangerous there.

Excavate To uncover something buried, by digging away and removing the earth around it.

Extinct A volcano that will never erupt again.

Fertile Land that is good for growing crops and plants.

Gas A substance, such as air, that will spread to fill any space that contains it.

Geological Having to do with Earth's physical structure, especially its layers of rock.

Lava The hot, liquid rock that pours out of a volcano when it erupts. Also, the rock formed when this liquid has cooled and hardened.

Magma Melted rock found beneath Earth's surface that becomes lava when it flows out of volcanoes.

Mineral A solid substance found in the earth that does not come from an animal or plant.

Roman A person who lived in ancient Rome, or anything having to do with the people or culture of ancient Rome.

Shock wave A disturbance caused by an earthquake or explosion that travels through the ground, sea, or air.